A ROOKIE READER

A PEAR
BY ITSELF

Written and illustrated
by Bonnie Jeanne Baker

Prepared under the direction of Robert Hillerich, Ph.D.

CHILDRENS PRESS ™

CHICAGO

For Robbie

Library of Congress Cataloging in Publication Data

Baker, Bonnie Jeanne.
  A pear by itself.

  (A Rookie reader)
  Summary: Rhyming text and illustrations
describe what makes up a pair. Includes a
word list.
  1. Vocabulary—Juvenile literature.
[1. Vocabulary]   I. Title.   II. Series.
PE1449.B28   428.1   82-4430
ISBN 0-516-02032-3   AACR2

A pear by itself is not a pair.

4

It takes two to make a pair.

It doesn't matter what you choose.

It's a pair if it comes in twos.

Some things always come in twos.

8

You'd look pretty funny
with just one shoe!

One trouser leg is not a pair.

Only half of it is there.

Butterflies need a pair of wings.

So do birds...

...and other things!

14

Sometimes people come in pairs.

16   Twins are a pair

because two are there. 17

A bride and groom

are a pair who care.

19

A mommy and daddy

are a pair who share.

One dog by itself is not a pair.

Add one more and a pair is there.

Two hares in two chairs

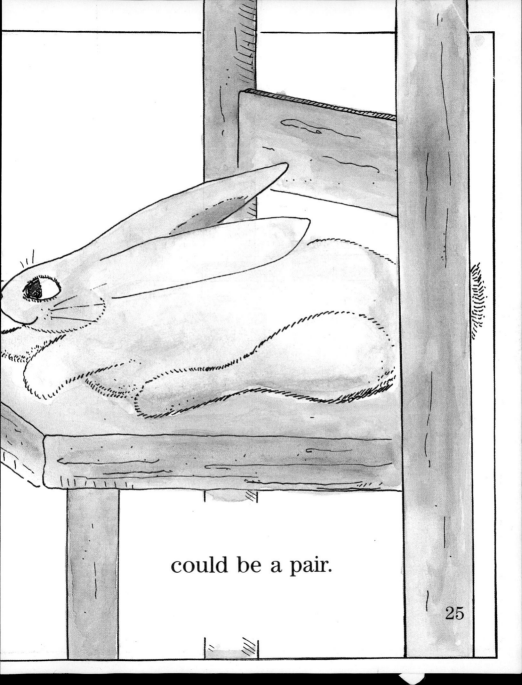

could be a pair.

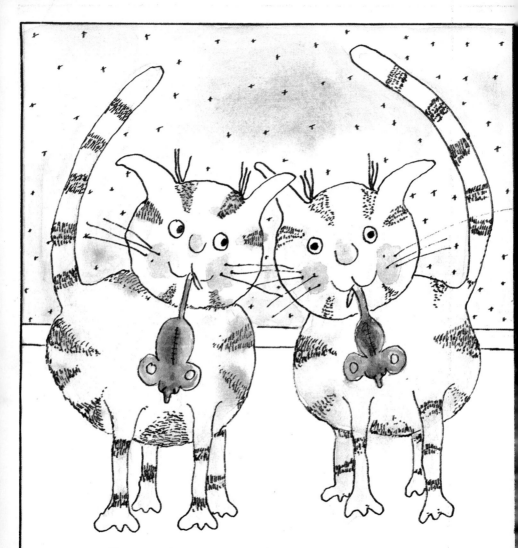

Just about anything could be a pair.

Even two pears could be a pair.

Have you ever eaten
a pair of pears?

WORD
LIST

a	by	even
about	care	ever
add	chairs	funny
always	choose	groom
and	come	half
anything	comes	hares
are	could	have
be	daddy	if
because	do	in
birds	doesn't	is
bride	dog	it
butterflies	eaten	it's

itself	other	there
just	pair	things
leg	pairs	to
look	pear	trouser
make	pears	twins
matter	people	two
mommy	pretty	twos
more	share	what
need	shoe	who
not	so	wings
of	some	with
one	sometimes	you
only	takes	you'd

About the Author-Artist

Bonnie Jeanne Baker lives and teaches art in Atlanta. She received a Master's degree in Art Education from Florida State University and has taught all ages in both public and private schools. She presently teaches at the American College for the Applied Arts and DeKalb Community College. She also gives private art lessons to her favorite age group, small children.